Scrappy Quilts Handbook

A Guide to Get Creative Using Your Leftover
Stashes and Fabrics in Quilting Scrap Quilt Patterns
and Projects

By

Zera Meyer

Disclaimer

This book offers knowledgeable and trustworthy information on the subject area discussed. Nevertheless, the opinions presented in this work belong solely to the author and are not intended to be considered expert advice or counsel. The reader is therefore accountable for his/ her own decision.

Contents

Introduction

Learning to build a scrap quilt is simple and empowering because it relieves the pressure of choosing colors for your project. Instead, you will concentrate on selecting fabrics that stand out from one another, and the finished project will still be stunning, even if a few of your selections weren't precisely what you had in mind.

Making a quilt block—or even sections of quilt blocks—at once is totally acceptable, regardless of the style of quilt you intend to make. Get a box to retain your ongoing project, adding to it as you get additional fabric scraps to play with.

Once you are set to begin organizing your quilt, the blocks or other pieces should be placed on a design wall. Any visible wall will do just fine; a fancy wall is unnecessary. Most quilters move patchwork or other pieces here and there until they're pleased with the layout of a scrap quilt. Being successful at scrap quilting takes practice, just like any other type of quilting, so consider the tip provided here as a start-off point to assist you in making a quilt that's rich with visualization; however, there are a lot more you need to know before making a scrap quilt, hence the purpose of this book.

So, let's get started!

What are Scrap Quilts?

Scrap quilts are quilts formed from a random collection of fabrics, i.e., as though the quilter closed his/ her eyes to select the assortment of fabrics. The truth is that some thought goes into your choice of fabric; however, it is more of color value and dominance than the actual color itself.

According to traditional quilting origin, most scrap quilts were "make-do" projects made from leftover pieces so as to be frugal in using every fabric scrap there is. Several scrap quilts were undoubtedly made like that, particularly in difficult times, but also possibly quilted by quilters who purely adored sewing with various fabrics.

Nowadays, it's common for quilters to have a ton of leftover fabric hanging around so that they have everything they'll require at hand for a scrap quilt the next time a pattern catches their attention.

Sourcing for Scrap Fabrics

The pieces of fabric left upon completing a project are perfect for making scrap quilts. However, if you don't have sufficient fabric scraps to make a scrap quilt, what then? Perhaps you need to add some beloved patterns that aren't already in your fabric stash, widen your scrap collection, or even round out your stash's colors and values. Whatever the case may be, I'll outline some approaches to getting scraps for your next scrap quilt.

But first!...

When I first learned to quilt years ago, I wanted to sew a quilt for my unborn child. I owned three blue fat quarters, yet I needed to use a variety of blue fabrics, and buying ten more was not in my budget. I, therefore, did what every new mother would do and called my mother. Although my mother doesn't quilt, she sews clothes, so I was certain she had some blue fabric. I believed she could assist me because all I needed was 2 ½" squares, and she obliged. Some days later, a delivery containing more than sufficient blue fabric pieces to complete my quilt showed up at my door.

The leftover fabric was a lifesaver, and I've been sewing scrap quilts since then.

Below are some methods for sourcing scraps if you don't have an overflowing basket of scrap fabrics.

- **Ask Around for the Exact Scrap Fabrics**

Before we begin with this, remember that you shouldn't count on other quilters to offer all the fabric needed for your scrap quilt, not even to share. However, people are frequently eager to give their leftovers if they're no longer needed. Okay, let's keep going!

Nothing works better than simply asking your quilting fellows for some scraps. If you are open to accepting anything or understand exactly what you're looking for, this method will work quite effectively. Remember I previously requested the blue fabric scraps from my mother and not the generic scraps.

Request for fall colors if you want to sew a quilt that has fall leaves to enhance the leaves' variation. Or perhaps you're seeking any 1930s-era fabric. If you are certain of what you need, be explicit in your request; if not, be generic in your request.

- **Try to Use Precuts**

Precuts were not all that popular when I started making my quilts. Simply put, they were not as widespread in the early 2000s. Nonetheless, precuts are an excellent way of getting various prints together. Precuts are essentially individual chunks of a fabric range or collection and are a simple method to diversify your scrap collection. Charm packs, mini charm bundles, jelly rolls, layer cakes, etc., will help in adding some variety to your scrap collection.

If you choose to use precuts, you should incorporate different fabrics so that the precuts wouldn't make a scrap quilt look excessively color-coordinated. Your quilt will seem scrappy but coherent if precuts are used for half of the fabric and complementary scraps for the other half. My preferred kind of scrap quilt!

- **Conduct a Scrap Trade**

I enjoy trading scraps! It feels good to get rid of certain scraps I don't use or desire to keep, and it's a lot of pleasure to discover lovely pieces among other quilter's scraps. We do a scrap trade every year during our group getaway, and it is interesting to see everyone dig through the scraps to select their preferences. You can host your own group scrap trade or invite a few friends over for a little trade. Everyone can go home with some goodies! If you're unable to organize a scrape trade, you can partake in one held by scrap trade communities.

You can also grab scraps off the ground or from trash cans at sewing retreats. Yes, a quilt can dazzle even with little bits of scraps. I am frequently shocked by the sizes of fabric some people throw away in the trash can.

- **Thrift Store**

Go to your neighborhood thrift store; you could find some fabric if you get lucky.

- **Get a Scrap Pack of Fabric From Your Local Quilt Shop, eBay or Etsy**

Do the quilt shops in your area sell scrap bags? There may be some nice fabric at discounted prices there. Several people offer fabric scrap packs for sale on eBay or Etsy. Ensure you thoroughly read the description before making an online purchase to be certain of what you are receiving. Sometimes the picture of the scrap pack will give you an idea of the fabrics you might get, but it's not always an exact match of what you will receive.

- **Freecycle**

A forum that is arranged by location is called Freecycle (freecycle.org). You can make an "Offer" on the website if you have anything to give away, and you can make a "Wanted" post if you're searching for something. Despite the hit-or-miss nature of this, it can't hurt to advertise your search for fabric scraps.

You should now have some nice ideas and starting points for your search for fabric scraps. Nothing is finer than a patchwork scrappy quilt! Best of luck with your hunt for scraps!

Sorting and Organizing Scrap Fabrics

When it comes to scrap pieces, being able to sort and store them in an orderly arrangement is the most frequent challenge. Even though some sewers opt to retain even the smallest piece of scraps while others only retain the bigger pieces, the issue of keeping the scraps organized and accessible remains the same. Below are some ideas to help you sort and organize all your scrap pieces in an orderly manner.

Sorting Your Scrap Fabrics

Here are some scrap sorting tips to get you started.

- Cut them first into sizes and shapes that are suitable for use

Start with your biggest pieces first. Consider how you will cut the scraps. Starting at the selvage and cutting throughout the fabric's width produces the best size of strips. Cut strips that are 1 ½, 2, and 2 ½ inches in width. These strips work well when used to quilt blocks of log cabins and rail fences. Alternatively, you can decide to cut them into square or rectangular pieces for blocks of Chevron, 4-patch, or 9-patch.

- Sort pieces by size and color

Sorting your stockpile of fabric scraps by size can help you get it started with its organization. They can first be arranged into three groups: small, smaller, and smallest. After that, group them according to color. However, it would be better not to separate your scraps by color if you're primarily a quilter and infrequently quilt with a particular color because you'll have to search through too many bags or baskets to get the size you want.

- Iron your scraps

The time saved by not having to dig amongst entangled and ruffled pieces every time you begin a project may be the biggest benefit of having your fabric scraps tidy and ironed. All you need to do is to select the pieces you want and begin sewing.

Organizing Your Scrap Fabrics

Once you've sorted your scraps, try one of these methods below to have them stored.

1. Store them in transparent boxes or baskets. The ideal boxes to use are transparent ones so you can easily see the size and color of the pieces within. Labeling the baskets or boxes you choose to use will be helpful.

2. Cover your fabric scraps. The vibrant colors of your scrap stockpile will degrade if improperly stored, and it'll start to gather dust. Keep them in baskets, boxes, or other containers with lids, enclosures, or seals whenever feasible. If stored on a shelf, ensure they are kept away from your windows. When you're not engaged in a project, your shelf can be covered with a piece of fabric. This will assist you in keeping your scraps dust-free.

3. Consider using mason jars. Each jar should be filled with scraps of a specific color, and then the lid should be fitted to prevent spills.

4. Make use of the scraps in such a way as to store them. Create a patchwork piece of fabric out of your leftover scraps, and then stitch it into a storage box or basket to store additional leftovers.

5. Organize scraps into large zipped plastic bags according to type or color. After that, put them in a storage tote to keep them out of the sun.

6. Get a trolley that comes with a few tiny plastic compartments. Each compartment should be filled with pieces of the same color.

7. Utilize an old dresser as a system for storing your scrap fabrics. If the drawers are too big, partition them into segments with cardboard and place a different color in each one.

8. Use a shoe organizer that can be hung over a door or wall with multiple compartments. Scraps should be placed in each compartment.

9. Store your leftovers using under-the-bed storage boxes. They won't even be noticed by your spouse down there!

10. You can get stackable baskets from an office supply store. To conserve space, stuff the scraps into each one and stack them over each other.

Choosing Fabrics for Scrap Quilts

A particular type of fabric can be the foundation upon which you can build scrap quilts. Quilts constructed using a variety of batiks are one example, as are watercolor quilts, which are based on a wide range of floral patterns. No hard rule exists.

It's also entirely up to you how many fabrics you choose to use in your scrap quilts, from charm quilts—where it's the norm not to use a fabric more than once—to quilts that have a slightly more organized appearance.

Below are some of what you should keep at the back of your mind while preparing to quilt scrap quilts.

- The secret to building a stockpile of scrap quilt fabrics is variety. Select a variety of fabrics, including the ones you don't particularly fancy.

- Pick fabrics with a variety of colors. That entails embracing all of the rainbow colors, including light and dark colors, in addition to your faves.

- Incorporate neutral fabrics like white, cream, brown, and black. They provide a soothing spot for your eyes to rest and divide up patches of the quilt that may otherwise be so busy.

- Scrap quilts usually depend on contrast, value, and even color to convey a clear design. As a result, while employing a wide range of fabrics, you still want to ensure that the pattern's design is visible. To achieve the desired contrast, you should choose a variety of light, medium, and dark fabrics. Snap a photo of your fabrics on your phone, then turn the image to black and white if you aren't sure whether there is sufficient contrast. Add or remove fabrics and take many shots until you are satisfied with the outcome because if you don't notice a visible difference in the photo, you can have a mushy design in your quilt once completed.

- Don't forget to use tone-on-tone fabrics. These fabrics, also known as ToTs, frequently look solid from afar but are actually prints with two or more shades of the same color when viewed at close range. They make great blenders and may be used to give a quilt some element of contrast and variety.

- Anything can go when choosing fabrics for scrappy quilts. You can combine vintage and modern prints, go with stripes, florals, novelty, plaid, or geometric (the more diversity, the better), and incorporate tone-on-tones and batiks. Add some glitter, ensuring that around 25% of the medium/dark prints are lighter than the rest. Distribute the more colorful pieces of the quilt uniformly across the quilt.

- Use a single backdrop print instead of several prints if you want a more modest version of scrappy. Or choose a particular color scheme and gather fabric scraps that match that scheme. Your quilt will become a bit more organized as a result.

Getting Started to Sew with Your Scrap Fabrics

You've sourced your scrap fabrics, and every measure discussed in the previous sections is already well noted and actioned on, and now you are set to sew some lovely quilt designs with your scrap fabric. However, before you go all out to quilt that design, proper planning is essential if you want the best possible outcome for your scrappy project. Here are a few ideas to help you plan effectively for your scrappy projects.

1. Make a List

Keeping lists really does help me stay organized. Identify the fabrics in your stockpile that you intend to utilize. Include suggestions for potential uses for the fabric in your list. You might be thinking that it might work well for pillowcases. Or baby quilts. Or anything. However, if you don't document it, you might lose the rationale behind why you're storing that particular fabric.

2. Set Current Goals

Your sewing objectives need not be big or grandiose. I have had periods where I have considered myself successful if I complete just one scrap or stash project. Many people can sew quickly, so they may be capable of donating a baby quilt or large quilt every three months or more frequently throughout the year. Simply consider what you practically hope to accomplish and then set the target. When you complete your project, you will feel good about yourself.

3. Maintain a Bucket List of Scrap Projects

Keeping a list like this is wonderful. I will always find something interesting on my list to keep me inspired to sew whenever I feel stuck in a sewing rut. I generally keep stuff I contemplate using in a bunch of drawers, and I try to periodically look through them to generate ideas.

4. Establish a Routine For Handling Scraps

You will be far more able to keep up with your scraps if you set out a regular time each week or month to handle them. For me, I perform this scrap handling activity on the morning of each

Saturday. I occasionally only cut and store fabric scraps. And sometimes, I focus on working on some of my scrappy projects still ongoing. While on other days, I just review my notes to revise or adjust my goals. But even doing this feels fantastic! I only allot approximately an hour for this, and whatever more time I have for sewing is used for tasks on my current "to-do" list.

5. Sew Scrap Quilt Projects As You Work On Other Projects

After sewing my Harper's Garden fabric quilts a while back, I had a few hundred scraps left that could be quickly turned into half-square triangles, so I placed them beside my sewing machine, and I have been able to stitch each of the half-square triangles together during the last few months. The majority of the work is completed but still requires trimming. And all these sewings were done as I worked on other projects every now and then.

Scrappy Supplies and Materials

Below are the essential supplies and materials you need to make scrap quilts. These are my faves; however, you could choose to try out other various threads, rulers, and supplies to determine what works best for you.

Thread

For patchwork, consider using a cotton thread of the highest caliber. I prefer using tan or gray threads for assembling scrap quilts. These neutral tones go well with a variety of fabric hues.

Painter's Tape

With painter's tape, a provisional stitching guide can be made on your machine to prepare the quilt top for basting and stitching units of folded corners.

Tape Measure

Tape measure comes in very handy on the sides of a quilt when you want to add batting and borders or measure lengths of fabric.

Walking Foot

A walking foot is beneficial not just in machine quilting but also in binding your completed quilt. If a walking foot is not included as part of your sewing machine accessories, you can reach out to a nearby sewing machine operator to assist you in getting a walking foot that can work with your machine.

Acrylic Rotary Cutting Rulers

I suggest using a 6 by 24-inch ruler to snip across the fabric's width. A big square ruler (10-inches or more) is useful when you need to cut bigger pieces for blocks. A 6 ½-inch square 45-degree ruler is ideal when you want to mark stitching lines on units of folded corners, trim units of half-square-triangles, and crosscut strips into bite-sized chunks.

Sewing Machine and Needle

Periodically ensure you service your sewing machine and clean it frequently as directed by the manufacturer. For piecing, I prefer using an 80/12-sized sharp or multipurpose needle.

Pressing Iron and Board

Using a steam iron to press down a fabric before you cut is very essential. When assembling blocks, I ensure every seam allowance is pressed down neatly.

Scissors

Keep a tiny pair of scissors that's sharp by your sewing machine to cut threads.

Pins

Patchwork is best pinned using quilters or glass-head pins with a fine shank.

Rotary Cutter and Mat

If your rotary cutter's blade does not shut on its own while not in use, make it a practice to do so for safety reasons. Cutting will be far simpler if the blade is sharp. Employ a self-healing cutting mat while using a rotary cutter. To increase the lifespan of the rotary-cutter blade, ensure it's kept clean and dust-free

Seam Ripper

The seam ripper can be of any kind, so far it is very sharp to snip the thread without ruining the fabric.

Fine Mechanical Pencil

I like using this type of tool in fabrics of folded-corner units when I need to draw stitching lines.

Spray Starch

I apply spray starch on the scrap fabric before ironing to get rid of creases and provide body and rigidity before the fabric is cut into squares and strips. Spray starch becomes highly useful when stitching bias edges.

Scrappy Quilt Patterns and Projects

The quilt patterns below are examples of scrap quilt projects you can make using your scrap/ precut fabrics.

Scrappy Dice Quilt

I used yardage and fat quarters in this project, but scraps would also work just fine. Surely, you can use a range of prints to make your project appear more scrappy. This is an excellent way to use up your leftover fabrics. Charm squares (cut to 4 ½-inch square), mini charm squares, and any other fabric leftovers you have can be mixed and matched.

The linen-colored fabric in this project has an "X" shape inside of each block. The "X" shape brings to mind the number five on a dice, hence the project's name. The first thing you must choose is the accent fabric that will form the X in your project.

Materials

- 2 yards of accent fabric

- 140 4 ½" × 4 ½" squares in various prints (scraps, charm packs, etc.)
- 280 2 ½" x 2 ½" squares in various prints (scraps, charm packs, mini charm packs, etc.)
- 5 ¼ yards of backing fabric
- 3/4 yard of binding fabric
- 69 x 94-inch of batting fabric

Note: Cut the following measurement per print using the diagram below if you prefer using 18 fat quarters instead of scraps:

- 16 squares of 2 ½" x 2 ½" and;
- 8 squares of 4 ½" x 4 ½"

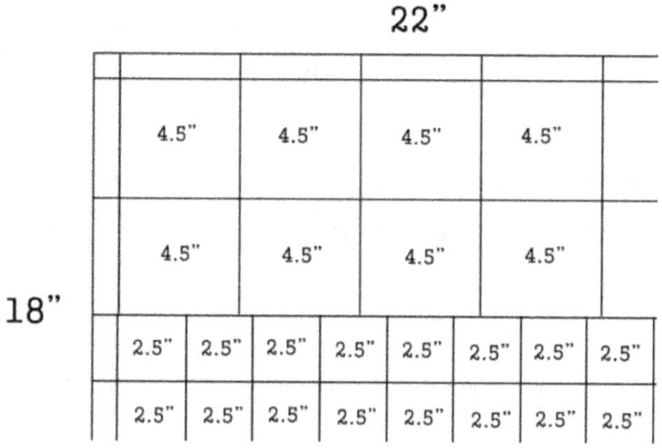

22"

4.5"	4.5"	4.5"	4.5"
4.5"	4.5"	4.5"	4.5"

18"

2.5"	2.5"	2.5"	2.5"	2.5"	2.5"	2.5"	2.5"
2.5"	2.5"	2.5"	2.5"	2.5"	2.5"	2.5"	2.5"

Finished Block: 12" x 12"

Finished Quilt: 60 ½" x 84 ½" (35 Blocks Set 5×7)

Instructions

Cutting

Cut the below measurements from the accent fabric:

- 5 strips 4 ½" x WOF. Subcut 35 squares 4 ½" x 4 ½" (8 for each strip).
- 18 strips 2 ½" x WOF. Subcut 280 squares 2 ½" x 2 ½" (16 for each strip).

Cut 8 strips 2 ½" x WOF fro the binding fabric

The Blocks

Assemble the following to make one block:

- 1 square 4 ½" x 4 ½" of accent fabric
- 8 squares 2 ½" x 2 ½" of accent fabric

- 4 squares 4 ½" x 4 ½" in various prints
- 8 squares 2 ½" x 2 ½" in various prints

Step 1: As per the illustration, assemble the accent print squares into the shape of an 'X.'

Step 2: Add (4) 4 ½" x 4 ½" of distinct squares to surround the central accent square.

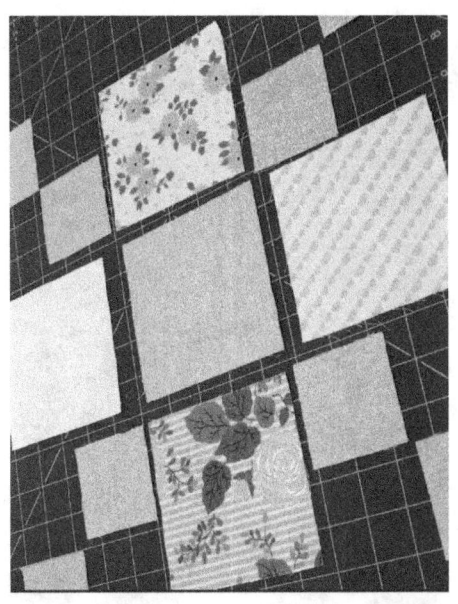

Step 3: Add the other (8) 2 ½" x 2 ½" distinct squares

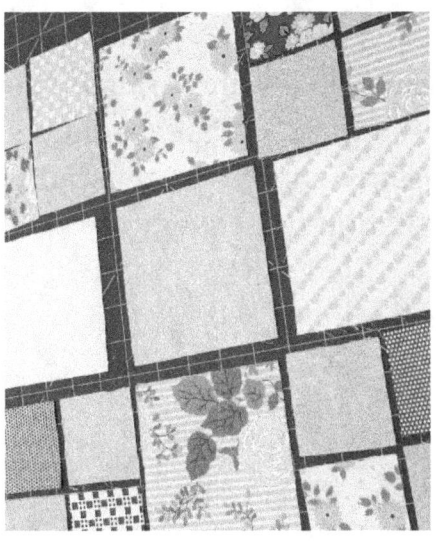

Step 4: Create 4-patch block units by sewing the 2 ½" squares together with a ¼" seam allowance.

Step 5: Make rows out of the units by sewing them. In order for the seams to "nest" seamlessly or lock into position, the seams should be pressed while changing the seams' orientation from row to row.

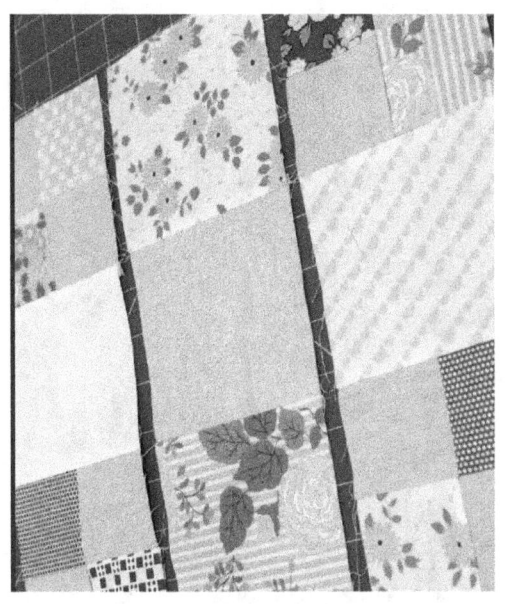

Step 6: Sew the rows to each other after aligning the seams and securing them in place, then press. The unfinished block should be 12 ½" by 12 ½" in size. I made 35 blocks.

Step 7: Organize them whichever way you prefer. I arranged my blocks into seven rows of five each.

After you've assembled it the way you prefer, the blocks should be sewn into rows; press (the orientation of the pressing should be alternated from row to row). Sew the rows to each other and press. My final quilt is 60 ½" x 84 ½" for the 5 by 7 setting.

Tip: If you choose to make an additional block (which would require 36 blocks altogether), this will make room for a 6 by 6 square quilt top, making the final quilt size measure 72 ½" by 72 ½". The fabrics would require a few modifications, but you would have sufficient backing, batting, and binding fabric.

Baste and bind the quilt as you'd normally do.

Scrappy Patchwork Quilt

You can sew a stunningly coordinated quilt using precut 2 ½" square pieces of fabric that are available in mini charm packs, or preferably, leftover scraps of fabrics can be used just as I did for this quilt pattern.

The fact that it is simple to determine the finished size of this patchwork quilt's single squares is yet another fantastic thing about this quilt. My 2 ½-inch pieces of fabric amount to 2-inch squares after sewing. I had the choice of making a quilt of whatever size, but upon cutting a significant number of squares, I chose to quilt 32 rows using 32 patches for every row.

Materials

- To exhaust more of my fabric scraps faster, I decided to use 2 1/2" squares of fabric for my quilt's top layer. 5" charm squares can likewise be used by simply cutting every single one into four pieces, or your squares can be cut from 2 1/2" strips of jelly roll in addition to the mini charm squares that have been neatly cut into 2 1/2".

- Keep some coordinating fabric aside for the binding
- 3 ½ yards of backing fabric

Finished Quilt: 64" x 64"

Instructions

Cutting

1024 squares of 2 ½ inches by 2 ½ inches each are needed for this quilt. There are several methods for cutting squares.

The simplest method is using a rotary cutter, ruler, and cutting mat that "self-heals" to cut several 2 ½ inch squares, or yet, the squares can be marked on the fabric using a pencil, then use scissors to cut them out.

I made my squares from my leftover fabric. Precut fabrics are another option, as was previously noted.

Assemble the Square Pieces

1. Two squares should be placed together with the right sides facing out, then sew one side with a seam allowance of ¼-inch.

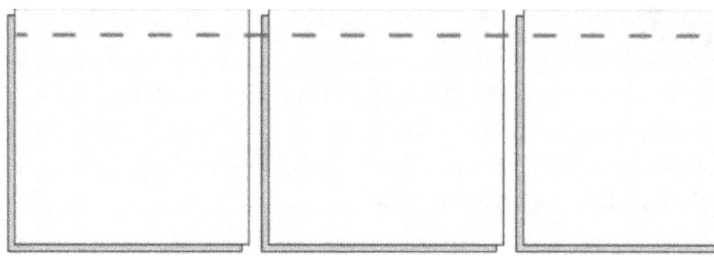

I enjoy chain piecing because it makes quilting more pleasurable and less difficult.

Chain piecing is when the patches' next set is sewn together before the thread is cut, and then removing the patches' first set from the sewing machine. You may continue sewing as many patches together as you please. I like to snip the chained pieces apart after pressing it on my ironing board.

A pile of chain-sewn squares

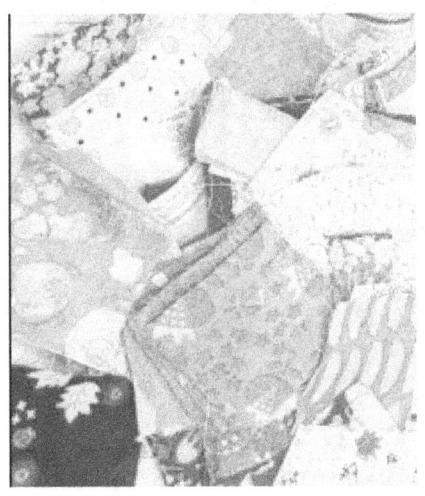

Squares being matched for sewing

The first thing is sewing pairs of the 1024 squares side by side as given below.

2. Your preference should determine whether the seams would be pressed open or to the side. After that, snip your chain-pieced patches apart. You'll now have 512 patches.

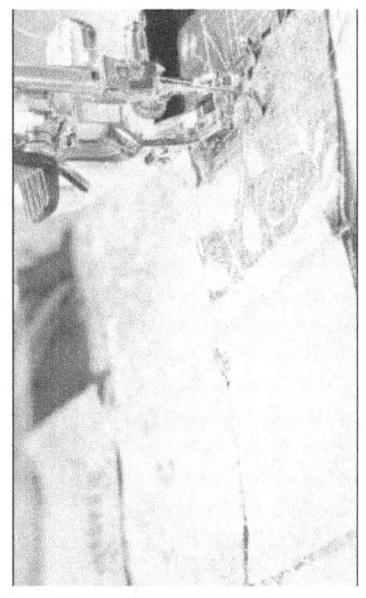

3. To form a small row of four squares, two patches' right sides should be placed together and one of the shorter edges' side should be sewn.

Keep chain piecing until you have sewn all the patches together. 256 small rows will be made by so doing. Then press open the seams or to one side

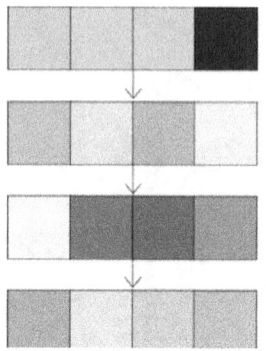 

4. Make a block of 16 patches by sewing four rows altogether.

To make 64 patch blocks, repeat the same as above. Then press open the seams or to one side

Making the Quilt Top

For the quilt top, the blocks of 16 patches should be sewn using a seam allowance of 1/4 –inch.

1. You can use a big leveled platform or a quilt wall design to organize the 64 blocks of quilt however you desire. Set up 8 rows with 8 blocks for every row.
2. Now, sew the blocks together in pairs. Keep sewing the pairs until you are left with 8 blocks in a row. Make 8 more rows by repeating this step.

3. Complete the quilt top by sewing the rows together, then press

Finishing

1. Sew together a piece of fabric that is 66" x 66" in size at the very least (having 2" excess all around) for the quilt's back.

2. Baste the quilt top, backing, and the 66" × 66" piece of batting altogether after sandwiching them. Pin or fusible basting is my go-to technique for holding my sandwich layers together.
3. Quilt the top of the quilt using your preferred method.
4. Cut off any surplus quilt backing and batting.
5. 7 binding strips 2 ½" WOF should be cut and sewn together with diagonal seams. Secure the quilt's unfinished edges by binding it using your desired technique.

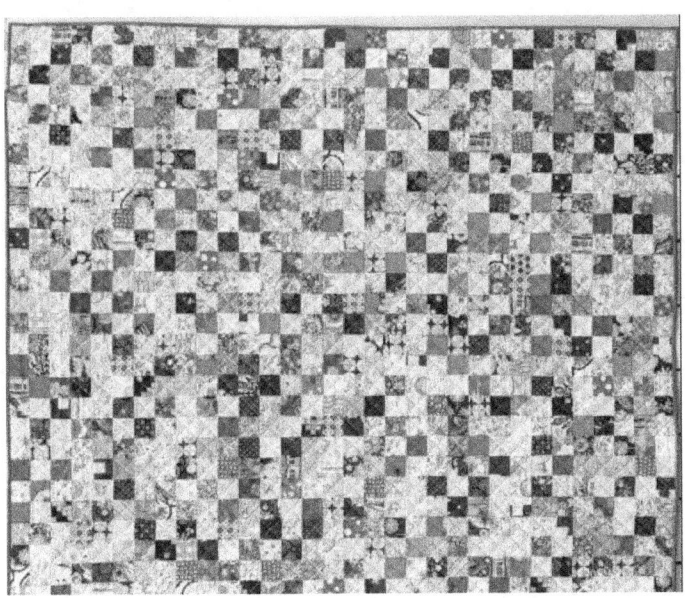

A Request from the Author:

Hey, I trust you're having a fascinating read. Please do share your feedback with me!

 I'd be forever thankful if you could spend only 60 seconds writing a brief product review of this book on Amazon.

>> To post a brief review, click here.

Thanks so much.

Scrappy Star Lap Quilt

This project is pretty exciting to make using only squares and half-square triangles, leaving you digging through your scrap pieces and getting into the scrap-busting mood!

Materials

- Scrap fabric of coordinating colors for the star lap quilt
- Keep some coordinating fabric aside for the binding
- Backing and batting fabric

Finished Block: 3" x 4"

No. of Blocks: 12 blocks of size 20"

Finished Quilt: 60" x 80"

Instructions

1. **Cutting**

You must first choose the size of the block you'd love to make. The block used in this project has a size of 20".

Dig through your fabric scraps and cut the exact quantity of squares shown for your preferred block size using the illustration below. If several blocks are to be made for the quilt top, the quantity should be multiplied by the number of blocks you wish to make.

Cutting Chart					
	Quanity	12" Blocks	16" Blocks	20" Blocks	24" Blocks
Low Volume Squares for HST	16	2 1/2" x 2 1/2"	3" x 3"	3 1/2" x 3 1/2"	4" x 4"
Grey Squares for HST	12	2 1/2" x 2 1/2"	3" x 3"	3 1/2" x 3 1/2"	4" x 4"
Color Squares for Star HST each square is a different color	8	2 1/2" x 2 1/2"	3" x 3"	3 1/2" x 3 1/2"	4" x 4"
Color Squares for Diamond HST each a different color - any color	4	2 1/2" x 2 1/2"	3" x 3"	3 1/2" x 3 1/2"	4" x 4"
Low Volume Squares	16	2" x 2"	2 1/2" x 2 1/2"	3" x 3"	3 1/2" x 3 1/2"
Color Squares for Star each squares is same color but different print of Color Squares for Star HST	8	2" x 2"	2 1/2" x 2 1/2"	3" x 3"	3 1/2" x 3 1/2"

2. Creating Half-Square Triangles (HSTs)

From left to right, sort the HST blocks you've cut into;

- 8 sets of the same color/ white sets,
- 8 sets of grey/ white, and

- 4 of any other color/ grey sets

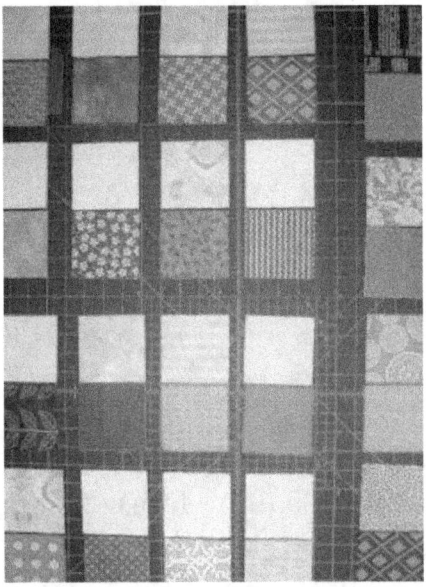

A time-saving tip is to make a whole quilt of blocks by repeating each step for HST in an assembly-line manner, as shown above.

A diagonal line should be drawn on the backside of the dark fabric, as shown below.

Place your dark square fabric scrap on top of your light square fabric with their right sides facing each other. Both sides should be pinned to the drawn line. Ensure to space them apart sufficiently so that your presser foot wouldn't run across them while sewing. Now, sew a ¼-inch seam allowance on the two sides of the line; your sewing lines are indicated by the black lines.

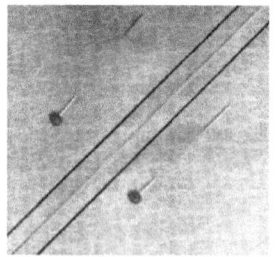

Thereafter, every set on the line's right side should be chain stitched, repeating the same for the ones on the left.

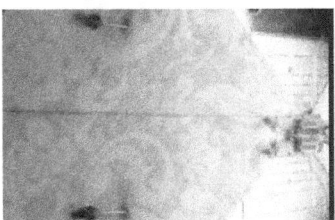

Snip your threads and position your ruler on the center line. Cut your fabric scraps apart following the center line.

Press in the direction of the dark fabric.

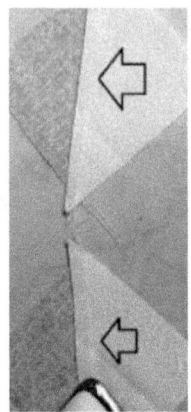

It's time for your HST to be trimmed. The trim sizes for every block size are as follows:

- A 12-inch block is a 2-inch square trim size
- A 16-inch block is a 2 ½-inch square trim size
- A 20-inch block is a 3-inch square trim size
- A 24-inch block is a 3 ½-inch square trim size

I'll utilize the 3-inch trim size for my demonstration. To begin, the HST's seam line should be aligned with the 45° mark on your ruler. Ensure that the HST's raw edges are above the 3-inch mark on your ruler. The two sides of the ruler's edge should now be trimmed.

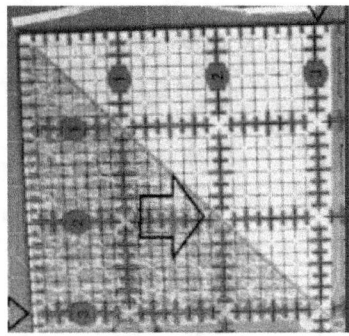

Turn your block to 180°. Again, the HST's seam line should be aligned with the 45° line on your ruler. Ensure that the HST's raw edges are below the 3-inch mark on your ruler. The two sides of the ruler's edge should now be trimmed.

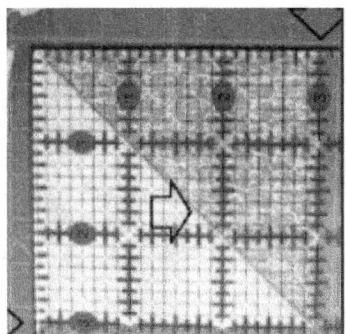

You should currently have an ideal half-square triangles.

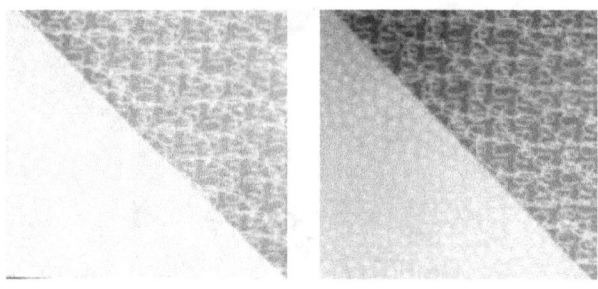

On the whole, there should be 40 half-square triangles.

3. Assembling the Star's Center Block Units

Lay down four sets of color/white half-square triangles in the following manner, using the corresponding color squares and four white color squares.

Sewing the squares into four quadrants of 4 at the beginning is, in my opinion, the simplest method to assemble the squares. With the right sides facing each other, begin stacking each row's first squares on the second squares and the third squares on the fourth squares, sewing a 1/4" seam allowance across all the corners (as seen in the top-left corner). Each quadrant's seams should be pressed in the reverse direction (as seen in the top-right corner). The top row should now be placed on the bottom row, one in each of the four quadrants. Pin the center seam into position after nesting it. A ¼" seam allowance should be sewn across each quadrant's pinned edge (as seen in the bottom-left corner), pressing to open the seams (as seen in the bottom-right corner).

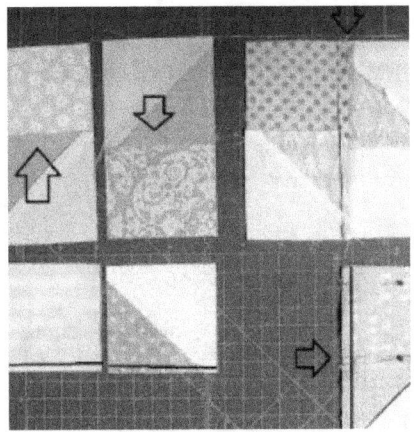

There should be four quadrants made up of four pieced squares. The four quadrants can now be stitched together.

With the right sides facing each other, stack the blocks on the left atop the blocks on the right. The center seam should be nested again, securing it in position with a pin. A ¼" seam allowance should be sewn across the pinned edge, pressing to open the seams.

Set the top row over the bottom row, ensuring their seams are aligned and secured into position. A ¼" seam allowance should be sewn across the pinned edge, pressing to open the seams.

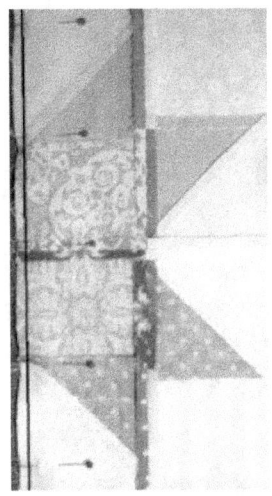

The center star is now completed! Keep this away for the time being.

4. Creating the Diamond Block's Points

It's time to make the diamond points. The procedure for turning quadrants into blocks, as previously done, is exactly the same approach we would adopt for the diamond points. Also, be aware that you'll be creating four diamond blocks; thus, working in an assembly-line manner will once more reduce the time spent.

Grab 4 grey/white HSTs plus 2 grey/color HSTs for every set, and arrange them as given below.

This time around, I layered the second squares in every row over the first squares and the fourth squares over the third squares, sewing a 1/4" seam allowance across the corners.

Each quadrant's seams should be pressed in the reverse direction. Afterward, the top row of both quadrants should be placed over the bottom row, nesting and pinning the center seam. A ¼" seam allowance should be sewn across the pinned edge, pressing to open the seams.

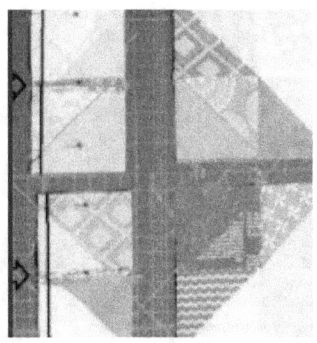

With the right sides facing each other, stack the blocks on the left atop the blocks on the right. The center seam should be nested again, securing it in position with a pin. A ¼" seam allowance should be sewn across the pinned edge, pressing to open the seams. Four of these units should be made, don't forget.

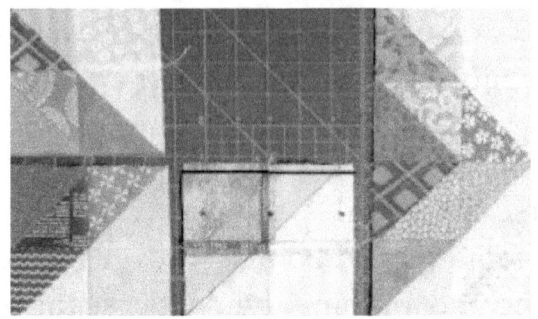

5. Creating the Corners for the Block

Lay out the other eight coordinating colored/white HSTs, four white squares, and four colored squares into four sets, as shown below.

The quadrants should be sewn like you previously did; first, sew the squares into rows, press them in reverse directions, and then sew the upper and bottom rows to each other, pressing to open the seam. A ¼" seam allowance should be used, and ensure your seams are nested.

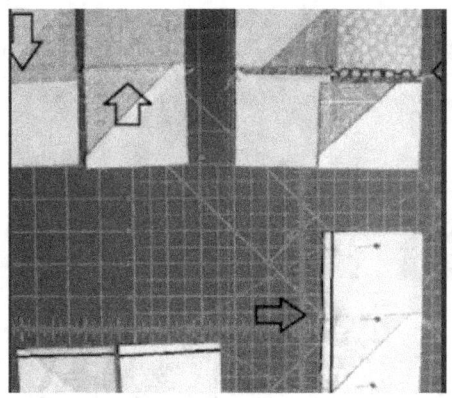

Four amazing corner blocks will be created afterward.

6. Stitching the Star Block

Organize your pieces as below.

With the right sides facing each other, each row's right-hand blocks should be stacked atop the center blocks. Your seams should be aligned and pinned into position. This should be repeated for the left-hand blocks. A ¼" seam allowance should be sewn across the pinned edge, pressing to open the seams.

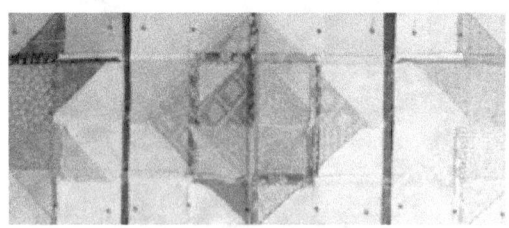

Three amazing rows will be created afterward

With the right sides facing each other, the top row should be stacked atop the center row. Your seams should be aligned and pinned into position. This should be repeated for the bottom row atop the center row. A ¼" seam allowance should be sewn across the pinned edge, pressing to open the seams.

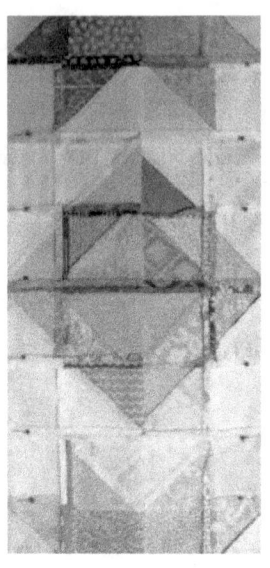

And now you have your lovely star lap block

Now, let's put some finishing touches on this scrappy quilt. Using my walking foot, I quilted some swirls all over the quilt to add brilliance. Don't forget to baste and bind the quilt as you'd normally do with your backing, batting, and binding fabric.

The last two projects are quite different from every other project discussed earlier, so let's try something different with our scrap fabrics.

Scrappy Potholder Quilt

This is your opportunity to make potholders if you've never done so. These potholders are suitable for my hands, measuring 7" x 7".

Materials

- 11 strips of fabric scraps
- Insulating fabric. You'll require (2) 8-inch squares
- 8 ½-inch square backing fabric
- Binding bias tape and hanging tag (if you choose to). Cut out 2 strips that measure 2 x 32-inches if you'd prefer to create your own bias tape. When creating your hanging tags (if you wish to), two extra 2 x 4-inch pieces should be cut.

Instructions

1. Print the templates below.

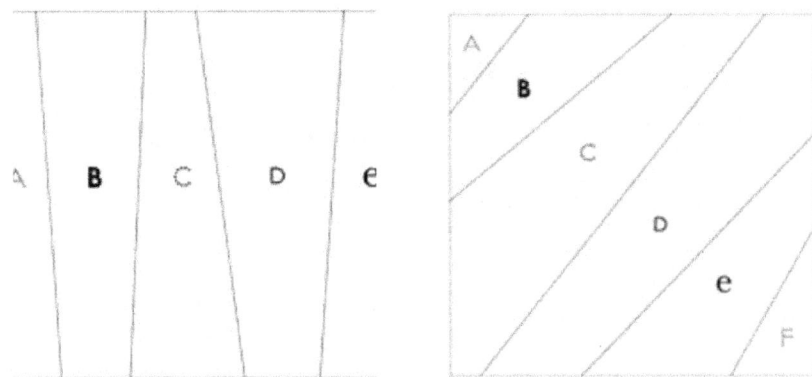

2. Choose a fabric scrap for every pattern, then make fabric cut-outs. You may simply draw the pattern pieces using a mechanical lead pencil or water-soluble marker, cutting them out with scissors. However, I used my rotary cutter and ruler in this case.

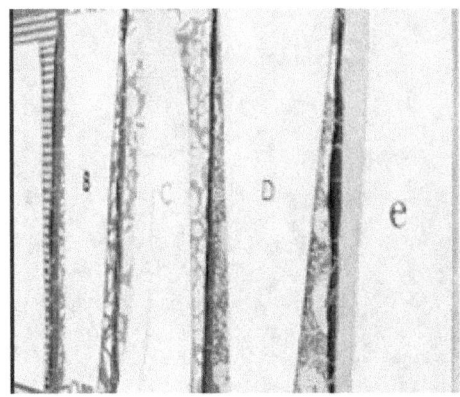

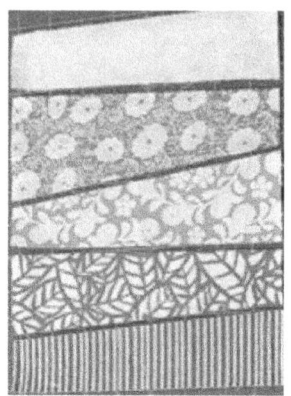

3. With a ¼" seam allowance, stitch the pieces together. Don't be bothered if your finished square's sides are not aligned. We'll surely trim them accordingly in the subsequent step upon squaring the blocks.

4. Square the completed blocks into seven squares

5. Assemble your quilt by sandwiching the backing fabric with the insulating material. You can also use the pinning method or spray adhesive.

 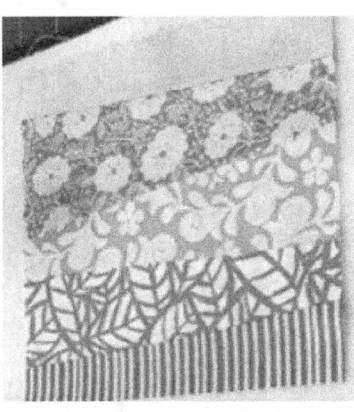

6. Be innovative when quilting your potholders. I used a stitch length of 3 on my machine to quilt haphazard straight lines to give it a more contemporary appearance. Trim off any excess fabric material.

 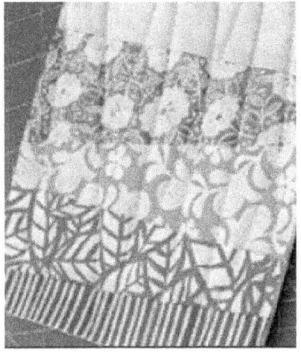

7. Make your bias tape, then attach the binding.

8. You can fix a hanger if you choose to by sewing it underneath the binding (to the edge). You could do this using a ribbon, coordinating fabric, or the selvage of a designer fabric. There you go, your two distinct potholders.

The End... Almost!

Hey! This book has come to its last chapter, and I trust you've had a good read thus far.

As a self-published author with a limited advertising budget, I depend on you, my readers, to post a quick review of my book on Amazon because readers hardly post reviews.

So, if you truly liked this book, would you kindly...

Submit a quick review on Amazon by clicking >> here.

Thanks so much.

Scrappy Coasters Quilt

These coasters are excellent, given that they're unbreakable and gentle on your table. In case there are any spills, you can easily have them washed.

Materials

- Batting scraps. You could create a square or rectangular coasters. My coasters were 5 × 5-inch in size. To factor in the seams, your completed coaster will be ½" smaller than your batting's size.
- Fabric scraps. To get started, you'll require a few small scraps for the center, and to complete the coasters, you'll require a few strips of fabric that are as long as your batting. Your scraps and strips should be at least an inch or wider for this coaster.
- Backing fabric. The size of the backing fabric should match that of your batting square when cut.

   N.B. If you'd prefer it to be really scrappy, you may need to piece the backing fabric using two or more scrap pieces.

Instructions

1. Choose a scrap fabric to start with. To start, you'd need a fabric scrap whose edges are straight to cater for the coaster's center, which can be of any form, such as trapezoid, square, triangle, hexagon, or any form whose sides are straight.

You can choose the size you want your starting scraps to be; I chose somewhere around 1" and 2 ½" in width for the above. The image above that appears to be two pieces is actually two fabric scraps already attached. However, for the sake of this instruction, consider it as a single unit.

The scrap fabric you are starting with should be placed anywhere on your piece of batting. Don't overthink it; simply put it anywhere. I placed mine in the middle.

The stitch length on your machine should be set to what you prefer using when quilting; In my case, a stitch length of 3 or 3.5 is typically used

Use straight, wavy, or free-form lines in quilting down the first fabric scrap. To attach the next fabric pieces, you should leave some room at the edges after quilting it just enough to secure it in position.

2. Continue quilting and add more scraps as you quilt. The next step is to sequentially add scraps on either side of the first scrap. Wherever you can, I consider it ideal if light and dark fabrics are alternated, regardless of if you're using a collection of coordinated fabrics or just completely random.

   Now, two scraps should be placed with their right sides together, with one scrap a bit longer than the other's straight edge, sewing with a ¼" seam allowance through the raw edge.

Your normal stitch length for piecing should be used rather than the longer stitch length of 3 or 3.5 for quilting (I typically step down to a stitch length of 2 when piecing - this is preferable when you need to join).

Afterward, the scrap should be flipped with the right side facing upwards, pressing the seam with your fingers.

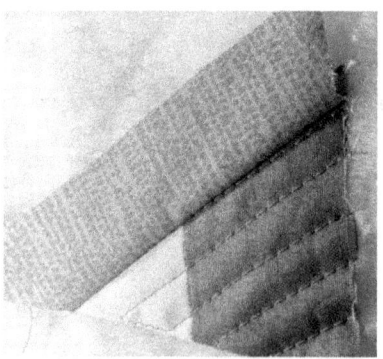

If the new scrap fabric piece just sewn is significantly longer than the first one, your scissors should be used to snip off the surplus before quilting it down similarly to the first piece of scrap fabric - this ensures that there are few bulk of scraps while going around.

Repeat the previous steps across all the first fabric scrap's sides, extending the subsequent scrap every time to completely enclose the subsequent straight line's raw edge. As a result, scrap 3 would be stitched over the joint edge of scraps 1 and 2.

Keep going around in this manner while you join and quilt along the way until your batting square is completely covered.

3. Cut off any extra scraps protruding beyond the batting square's edge.
4. Get your backing fabric piece which should be similar in size to your completed coaster's top, and have their right sides placed together.

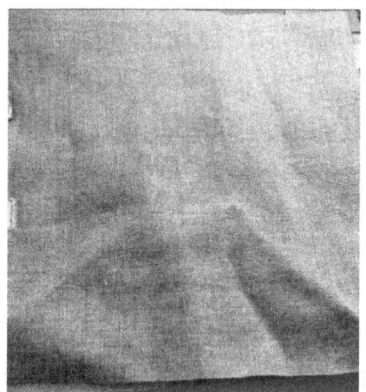

Use a seam allowance of ¼-inch to sew all across, providing a 2 to 3-inch space for turning. Any surplus fabric in the seams should be trimmed to simplify turning the right sides out and achieving sharp corners.

5. With your turning space, the right side of your coaster should be turned out, and pull the corners out with a blunt, pointed tool (such as the base of a thin paintbrush or a chopstick).

The raw edges of the turning gap/space should be turned in

The tuning gap's raw edges should be turned in while pressing your coaster with iron. Your coaster should be closed up as close to the edge (where feasible) by topstitching it using your desirable quilting stitch length. Take it slow as you move around the corners. Making a stitch over every corner is preferable to give it a slightly sharp corner.

And here is your finished coaster. You can also play around with different shapes; there is no limit to what you can make with your scrap fabrics.

Conclusion

Scrap quilts are incredibly well-loved among quilters. You already know that quilting is pricey. These supplies —fabric, thread, machines, rulers, etc.—cost a lot, and we need to stretch the cost it took to get them as much as possible to serve us well. Scrap quilting enables us to get the most from our investments, with scrap quilting patterns also providing extra benefits, such as the flexibility to exercise our quilt design skills to create stunning one-of-a-kind scrap quilts.

So, save your scrap pieces and get busy putting them to good use. I do hope you've had a wonderful and insightful read to help you make the best use of your scrap fabrics.

I wish you all the best in your scrappy quilts.